•••• BULLETPOINTS ••••

PREHISTORIC REPTILES

Andrew Campbell
Consultant: Steve Parker

Miles Kelly
PUBLISHING

First published in 2005 by Miles Kelly Publishing Ltd
Bardfield Centre, Great Bardfield
Essex, CM7 4SL

Some of this material also appears in the *1000 Facts* series and the *Visual Factfinder* series

2 4 6 8 10 9 7 5 3 1

Editorial Director: Belinda Gallagher

Editorial Assistant: Amanda Askew

Picture researcher: Liberty Newton

Production: Estela Boulton

Scanning and reprographics: Anthony Cambray, Mike Coupe, Ian Paulyn

British Library Cataloguing-in-Publication Data
A catalogue record for this book is available from the British Library

ISBN 1-84236-551-7

Printed in China

www.mileskelly.net
info@mileskelly.net

Contents

Reptile fossils

- **The first reptile** fossils exist in rock strata (layers) of the Carboniferous Period (355–298 mya).

- **The fossil record** for reptiles shows that all reptile groups – from pelycosaurs to dinosaurs – lived all over the world during their time.

- **Far fewer** early reptile fossils have been found in South America or Australia than in other parts of the world. Palaeontologists believe this is because they were not well preserved or have not yet been discovered.

- **Reptile fossils** can be preserved in very dry conditions, such as deserts, or can be buried under sediment.

- **Reptile fossils** discovered in desert conditions include entire dinosaur skeletons, found in sandstone in Mongolia.

- **The *Ichthyosaurus*** and *Plesiosaurus* fossils were discovered in Lyme Regis, England in the early 19th century. They forced many scientists to realize that creatures that had once existed had become extinct.

- **The fossil record** shows that numbers of flying reptiles and sea reptiles, together with some groups of dinosaurs, were in decline before the end of the Cretaceous Period (144–65 mya).

- **Messel**, near Frankfurt in Germany, is an important site for reptile fossils from the Early Tertiary Period, about 50 mya.

- **Reptile remains** from Messel include snakes, iguanas and an armoured lizard called *Xestops*.

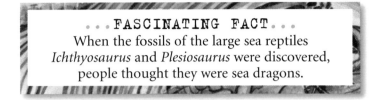

...FASCINATING FACT...
When the fossils of the large sea reptiles
Ichthyosaurus and *Plesiosaurus* were discovered,
people thought they were sea dragons.

▼ *The fossil remains of an* Ichthyosaurus, *showing the impression of its body in the rock. Many examples of* Ichthyosaurus *fossils have been discovered in rocks from the Jurassic Period (208–144 mya) in England and Germany.*

First reptiles

- **Reptiles** evolved from amphibians during the Carboniferous Period (355–298 mya).

- **Unlike amphibians,** which usually live near and lay their eggs in water, reptiles are much more adapted for a life on land.

- **Compared to amphibians**, reptiles had better limbs for walking, a more effective circulatory system for moving blood around their bodies, and bigger brains.

- **They also had more powerful** jaw muscles than amphibians and would have been better predators. Early reptiles ate millipedes, spiders and insects.

- **One of the earliest reptiles** was a small creature called *Hylonomus,* which lived in the Mid Carboniferous Period.

- *Hylonomus* lived in forests on the edges of lakes and rivers. Fossil remains of this reptile have been found inside the stumps of clubmoss trees.

- **Another early reptile** was *Paleothyris*. Like *Hylonomus*, it was about 20 cm long, and had a smaller head than amphibians.

- **One animal** that represents a staging post between amphibians and reptiles is *Westlothiana lizziae,* which was discovered in Scotland in the 1980s.

- *Westlothiana lizziae* lived in the Early Carboniferous Period (about 340 mya).

- **At first** palaeontologists thought that *Westlothiana lizziae* was the oldest reptile. But its backbone, head and legs are closer to those of an amphibian.

▶ Hylonomus, *meaning 'forest mouse', was one of the earliest reptiles. Fossil hunters discovered its remains in fossilized tree stumps at Joggins in Nova Scotia, Canada.*

Synapsids

- **Synapsids** were a group of reptiles that had a pair of openings on their lower skull, behind the eye socket, onto which their jaw muscles attached.

- **Synapsids** are the ancestors of mammals, which explains why they are sometimes called 'mammal-like reptiles'.

- **These reptiles** first appeared in the Late Carboniferous Period (about 310 mya). They became the dominant land animals in the Permian and Triassic Periods (298–208 mya).

- **The first synapsids** are called pelycosaurs. They were large, heavy-bodied animals that walked a bit like modern-day crocodiles.

- **The fierce meateater** *Dimetrodon* and the plant-eating *Edaphosaurus* – both of which had long, fanlike spines on their backs – were pelycosaurs.

- **Later synapsids** are called therapsids. The earliest therapsids had bigger skulls and jaws than pelycosaurs, as well as longer legs and shorter tails.

- **Later therapsids** are divided into two subgroups – dicynodonts and cynodonts. Dicynodont means 'two dog teeth' – cynodont means 'dog tooth'.

- **Dicynodonts** were herbivores. Most had round, hippopotamus-shaped bodies and beaks that they used to cut plant stems.

- **Cynodonts** were carnivores. They used different teeth in their mouth for different tasks – for stabbing, nipping and chewing.

- **Cynodonts** were the most mammal-like of all reptiles. Some had whiskers and may even have been warm-blooded.

▶ Diictodon *was a mammal-like reptile that lived about 260 mya. A plant-eater and a burrower,* Diictodon *was an advanced form of a synapsid known as a dicynodont.*

Moschops

- *Moschops* was a later synapsid reptile called a therapsid. It also belonged to a group of reptiles called dinocephalians (meaning 'terrible heads'), because it had a very big skull.

- **It was a plant eater**, and was probably preyed upon by large flesh-eating dinocephalians, such as *Titanosuchus*.

- *Moschops* lived in the Permian Period (298–250 mya) in southern Africa.

- **It grew up to 5 m long**. It had a squat body and a short tail. Stocky limbs held it well off the ground.

- *Moschops* had many peglike, chisel-edged teeth, which were adapted for biting and uprooting plant matter.

- **Its back** sloped downwards from the front, rather like a giraffe's.

- **It had enormous limb girdles** for both its front and rear legs, to support its heavy weight.

- *Moschops* had a high skull with a thick bone on top, which it may have used to head-butt its rivals or enemies.

- **Its skull bones** became thicker as it got older. This thickening of the skull is called pachyostosis.

- **While *Moschops'* skull** was very big, its brain was not. 'Bone head' might be a good nickname for it!

▼ *The bones on the top of Moschops' skull could be up to 10 cm thick – enough to withstand the blows from head-butting rivals or enemies.*

Cynognathus

- **Cynognathus** was a therapsid reptile called a cynodont.
- **It lived** in the Early to Mid Triassic Period (250–220 mya).
- *Cynognathus* was the size of a large wolf, and weighed between 40 and 50 kg.
- **Its skull** was about 40 cm long, and its total body length was around 2 m.
- **Like modern wolves**, *Cynognathus* was an active predator.
- *Cynognathus* had some very mammal-like features. Palaeontologists think it may have been warm-blooded, may have had hair on its skin, and may have given birth to live young.
- **One of the many features** *Cynognathus* had in common with mammals was a bony palate that separated the mouth from the nasal cavity, and allowed it to breathe while it was eating.
- **Its teeth** were similar to a dog's. It had incisors (front teeth) for cutting, canines (teeth next to incisors) for piercing and molars (cheek teeth) for slicing.
- **The legs** were designed for fast running – they were tucked underneath and close to its body unlike the legs of *Moschops,* which stuck out more at the sides.
- **Fossil skeletons of *Cynognathus*** have been found in South Africa. Palaeontologists think that it favoured hunting in dry, desert-like areas.

◀ Cynognathus *means 'dog jaw'. Like other synapsid reptiles, it had strong muscles for opening and closing its jaws, which made it a powerful killer.*

Crocodilians

- **The first crocodile-like reptiles** were called eosuchians, meaning 'dawn crocodiles'. They appeared in the Permian Period (298–250 mya).

- **The first true crocodiles** appeared at the end of the Triassic Period (about 215 mya). They were called protosuchians, and lived in pools and rivers.

- *Protosuchus* was, as its name suggests, a protosuchian. It had a short skull and sharp teeth, and would have looked quite like a modern crocodile.

- **Other early crocodiles**, such as *Terrestrisuchus*, looked less like modern crocodiles.

▲ Fossils of Protosuchus, *meaning 'first crocodile', have been discovered in Arizona, dating to around 200 mya. Although* Protosuchus *was similar to living crocodiles in many ways, its legs were much longer.*

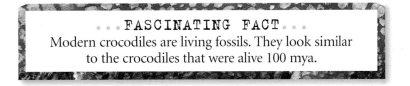

...FASCINATING FACT...
Modern crocodiles are living fossils. They look similar
to the crocodiles that were alive 100 mya.

- **Terrestrisuchus** had a short body and long legs. Its name means 'land crocodile', because palaeontologists think it may have been more at home on land than in water.

- **The next group** of crocodilians to evolve were the mesosuchians, which lived in the sea.

- **Metriorhynchus** was a marine mesosuchian. It had flippers instead of limbs, and very sharp, fish-stabbing teeth. It lived in the Late Jurassic Period (around 150 mya).

- **One subgroup** of mesosuchians, the eusuchians, are the ancestors of modern crocodiles.

  - **Deinosuchus** was an eusuchian. It was thought to be the largest-ever crocodile at 11 m long until a recent discovery of a *Sarchosuchus* fossil which is estimated to measure 15 m.

Archosaurs

- **The archosaurs** (meaning 'ruling reptiles') were a group of reptiles that came to dominate the land, seas and skies in the Mesozoic Era (250–65 mya).

- **Archosaurs** included crocodilians, dinosaurs and the flying reptiles called pterosaurs.

- **Archosaurs** are the ancestors of modern birds and crocodiles.

- **Archosaurs** were diapsid reptiles – they had two openings in the skull to which jaw muscles were attached, which meant their jaws were very powerful.

- **The first archosaurs** appeared in the Permian Period (around 255 mya). They would have looked quite like lizards, but with shorter bodies and longer legs and necks.

- **One early archosaur** was *Chasmatosaurus*. It had a large, heavy body, and probably spent most of its time hunting in rivers.

- *Lagosuchus* was another early archosaur. Some palaeontologists think it might have been the direct ancestor of the dinosaurs.

- *Lagosuchus* was very small. It was about 30 cm long and weighed about 90 g. It had a slender body, and ran on its hind legs.

- **The name** *Lagosuchus* means 'rabbit crocodile' – palaeontologists think it may have moved like a rabbit by hopping.

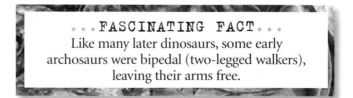

...FASCINATING FACT...
Like many later dinosaurs, some early
archosaurs were bipedal (two-legged walkers),
leaving their arms free.

16

▲ Chasmatosaurus *was an early archosaur and a forerunner of the dinosaurs. It lived about 250 mya and grew up to 2 m long.*

Turtles and tortoises

- **Turtles** and tortoises both have shells that cover and protect their bodies. Because of this, they both belong to a group of reptiles called chelonians.

- **Chelonians' shells** evolved from belly ribs that grew outside of their bodies.

- **The earliest** chelonian fossils come from the Triassic Period (250–208 mya). They have been found in Germany and Thailand.

- *Proganochelys* was a very early chelonian.

- *Proganochelys* had a well-developed, heavily-armoured shell, but palaeontologists think that it could not pull its head, legs or tail inside it.

- **The ability** to pull the head, legs and tail inside the shell is important for turtles and tortoises, because it provides them with maximum protection.

- **The protective shells** of turtles and tortoises may have helped them survive at the end of the Cretaceous Period, 65 mya, when so many other reptiles became extinct.

- **Tortoises** have bigger shells than turtles. This is because tortoises are very slow-moving land creatures – unlike the swimming turtles – and need more protection.

- **A huge number** and variety of turtle fossils have been discovered at Riversleigh in Australia, dating from the Miocene Epoch (25–4 mya).

> ...FASCINATING FACT...
> Turtles and tortoises evolved a toothless
> beak for slicing meat or plants.

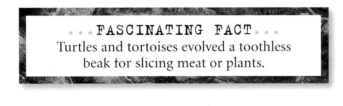

◄ Proganochelys, *an ancestor of modern turtles and tortoises, had a 60-cm-long shell, but it was unable to pull its head or legs inside.*

Archelon

▲ Archelon *fossils show that it was similar to, but much bigger than, modern leatherback turtles. Its front limbs were thinner and longer than its hind ones and were of more use to it in the water. Females used their back limbs to dig nests for their eggs, which they laid on land.*

> . . . FASCINATING FACT . . .
> Archelon means 'ruling turtle'. It could
> measure over 4 m in length, and was twice
> the size of modern turtles.

- *Archelon* was a giant sea turtle and the largest turtle ever to have lived.

- **It lived** in the seas off North America during the Cretaceous Period (144–65 mya).

- **It weighed** about 2.3 tonnes and fed on the different types of squid that swam in the Cretaceous seas.

- *Archelon* had very powerful front flippers that propelled it through the water.

- **Like other turtles** and tortoises, *Archelon* had a thick, bony shell to protect it.

- **Some experts** suggest that this shell was actually made of thick leather, to help give Archelon added buoyancy in the water.

- **The largest** *Archelon* skeleton was found in South Dakota, USA, in the mid-1970s. It now stands in the National Natural History Museum in Vienna, Austria.

- **The Vienna specimen** is 4.5 m long from beak to tail and 5.25 m wide from the end of one outstretched front flipper to the end of the other.

- **This turtle** was approximately 100 years old when it died, during a period of hibernation. It was then buried in mud on the sea floor.

Snakes

▲ *Some scientists argue that modern snakes, like this mangrove snake, are related to the prehistoric sea reptiles, mosasaurs. Like snakes, mosasaurs' limbs were reduced in size, and their bodies were long and flexible.*

- **The first-known snake** is *Dinilysia*, which was found in Argentina and lived in the Mid-Cretaceous Period, about 80 mya.

- **There are earlier** snakelike fossils, but palaeontologists generally think these were reptiles and not snakes.

- **The ancestor** of snakes was a lizard. Palaeontologists think it would have been a varanid lizard, of which the modern monitor lizard is an example.

- **Snakes** are an evolutionary triumph. They are one of the few land-living animals to survive – in fact to flourish – without arms or legs.

- **Compared to other reptiles**, snake fossils are rare. This is because snake bones are delicate and do not fossilize well.

- **Snakes evolved** into a huge variety of types in the Tertiary Period (65–1.6 mya). Today, there are more than 2000 snake species, living in nearly every type of habitat.

- **The 50 million-year-old fossil** finds from Messel in Germany include the remains of *Palaeopython*, an early python that grew to 2 m long.

- **Early snakes** killed their prey by strangling or squeezing them to death. Modern boas and pythons also use this method to hunt.

- **Poisonous snakes**, such as vipers, adders and cobras, did not evolve until the Miocene Epoch (25–4 mya).

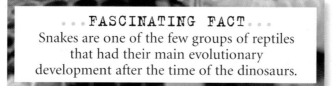

. . . FASCINATING FACT . . .
Snakes are one of the few groups of reptiles
that had their main evolutionary
development after the time of the dinosaurs.

Placodonts

- **After adapting** so well to life on land, some groups of reptiles evolved into water-dwelling creatures.

- **Placodonts** were early aquatic (water-living) reptiles. They lived in the Mid Triassic Period (about 240–220 mya).

- **The name placodont** means 'plate tooth'. These reptiles had large cheek teeth that worked like large crushing plates.

- **Placodonts** appeared at about the same time as another group of aquatic reptiles, called nothosaurs.

- **They had shorter**, sturdier bodies than the nothosaurs but, like them, did not survive as a group for a very long time.

- *Placodus* was a placodont. It had a stocky body, stumpy limbs, and webbed toes for paddling. It may have had a fin on its tail.

▶ Placodus *grew up to 2 m long, and probably used its sticking-out front teeth to scrape up molluscs from the seabed. Its platelike side teeth would then make short work of crunching the molluscs.*

- *Placodus* means 'flat tooth'. It probably used its flat teeth, which pointed outwards from its mouth, to prise shellfish off rocks.
- *Psephoderma* was a turtle-like placodont. Its body was covered in a shell, which in turn was covered by hard plates.
- *Psephoderma* also had a horny beak, like a turtle's, and paddle-shaped limbs.
- *Henodus* was another turtle-like placodont. It also had a beak, which it probably used to grab molluscs from the seabed.

Nothosaurs

- **Nothosaurs** were another group of reptiles that returned to live in the seas.

- *Nothosaurus* was, as its name implies, a nothosaur. Its neck, tail and body were all long and flexible.

- **Its total length** was about 3 m and its approximate weight was 200 kg.

- **Impressions** left in some *Nothosaurus* fossils show that it had webs between its toes.

- *Nothosaurus'* **jaw** had many sharp, interlocking teeth, which would have crunched up the fish and shrimps on which it fed.

- *Ceresiosaurus* was another nothosaur. Palaeontologists think it swam by swaying its body and tail from side to side, like a fish.

- *Ceresiosaurus* means 'deadly lizard'. It was bigger than *Nothosaurus* at 4 m in length and 90 kg in weight.

- **Nothosaurs emerged** in the middle of the Triassic Period (250–208 mya), but were extinct by the end of it.

- **The place left by the extinct nothosaurs** was taken by the plesiosaurs – another group of marine reptiles, but ones that were better adapted to life in the seas.

◀ Nothosaurus *was an aquatic reptile that could use its webbed feet to move over land. The long-necked nothosaurs were probably the ancestors of plesiosaurs, many of which also had long necks.*

.....FASCINATING FACT.....
Nothosaurus had nostrils on the top of their snouts, which suggests that they came to the water's surface to breathe, like crocodiles.

Ichthyosaurs

- **Ichthyosaurs looked similar** to sharks, which are fish, and to the later dolphins, which are mammals. When one type of animal evolves to look like another, scientists call it convergence.

- **Unlike plesiosaurs**, which relied on their paddles to propel them forwards, ichthyosaurs swayed their tails from side to side, like fish.

- **Hundreds of complete skeletons** of the ichthyosaur *Ichthyosaurus* have been discovered. This reptile could grow up to 2 m long, and weighed 90 kg.

- *Ichthyosaurus* had very large ear bones, which it may have used to pick up underwater vibrations caused by prey.

- **Some fossilized skeletons** of *Ichthyosaurus* and other ichthyosaurs have embryos (unborn infants) inside. This shows that ichthyosaurs gave birth to live young, as opposed to laying eggs.

- **One of the largest ichthyosaurs** was *Shonisaurus*, which was 15 m long and weighed 15 tonnes.

- **Ichthyosaurs** were plentiful in the Triassic and Jurassic Periods (250–144 mya), but became rarer in the Late Jurassic and in the Cretaceous Periods (144–65 mya).

- **Ichthyosaur** means 'fish lizard'.

- **Fossil-hunters** have found ichthyosaur remains all over the world – in North and South America, Europe, Russia, India and Australia.

▼ *Fossils of prehistoric marine reptiles such as* Ichthyosaurus *created a sensation in the early 19th century because fossil hunters discovered them before they had found any dinosaur remains.*

...FASCINATING FACT...
The first *Ichthyosaurus* fossil was found in 1811 by the English fossil-hunter Mary Anning. It took seven years before scientists identified the skeleton as that of a reptile.

Mosasaurs

- **Mosasaurs** were another group of large sea reptiles. They appeared between 160 and 120 mya, at the time when ichthyosaurs were less common.

- **Mosasaurs** were diapsid reptiles, a group that included dinosaurs and pterosaurs. All other large sea reptiles belonged to another group, the euryapsids.

- **Unlike the other** giant prehistoric sea reptiles, mosasaurs have living relatives. These include monitor lizards, such as the Komodo dragon.

- **The best-known mosasaur** is *Mosasaurus,* which could be up to 10 m long and 10 tonnes in weight.

- **The huge jaws of *Mosasaurus*** were lined with cone-shaped teeth, each of which had different cutting and crushing edges. They were the most advanced teeth of any marine reptile.

- **So distinctive** are *Mosasaurus'* teeth that palaeontologists have identified its tooth marks on the fossils of other animals, in particular the giant turtle *Allopleuron.*

- **The jaws of a *Mosasaurus*** were discovered in a limestone mine in Maastricht, in the Netherlands, in 1780. The fossil disappeared in 1795 when the French invaded Maastricht, but later turned up in Paris.

- **At first,** scientists thought the jaws belonged either to a prehistoric whale or a crocodile, until they decided they were a giant lizard's.

- ***Mosasaurus*** means 'lizard from the River Meuse', because it was discovered in Maastricht in the Netherlands, through which the River Meuse flows.

- **In 1998,** more than 200 years after the discovery of the first Mosasaurus fossil, palaeontologists discovered the remains of another Mosasaurus in the same location – the St Pietersburg quarry in Maastricht.

▼ Mosasaurus *was a fast swimmer. It had an enormous tail and paddle-shaped limbs, which it probably used as rudders.*

Gliding reptiles

- **One theory** about how reptiles became able to fly is that they evolved from reptiles that were able to glide.

- **Gliding reptiles** were tree-dwellers that jumped from tree to tree and developed a flap of skin that they used like a parachute – to help them soar and to break their fall.

- **Gliding between trees** saves time and energy and avoids the ground between trees, where predators may be lurking.

- *Coelurosauravus* was a tree-dwelling reptile of the Late Permian Period (260–250 mya).

- **The flaps of skin** that *Coelurosauravus* used for gliding stretched over long rods that grew out of the side of its body. Like wings, they could be folded away after use.

- **Palaeontologists** think that *Coelurosauravus* was an ancestor of the modern flying lizard, *Draco volans*, which lives in Southeast Asia.

- *Scleromochlus* was another gliding reptile. It lived in the Late Triassic Period, about 210 mya.

- *Scleromochlus* was about 20 cm long, with long, delicate back legs. It may have had flaps of skin on the sides of its body that would have worked like parachutes – just like those of modern flying squirrels.

- *Sharovipteryx* was another Late Triassic gliding reptile, the remains of which have been found in Central Asia.

- **Like *Scleromochlus***, *Sharovipteryx* had a lightweight frame and long back legs, but fossils indicate that there was also a flap of skin between its long back legs and its tail.

▼ Coelurosauravus, *which was around 60 cm long, lived in forests in Europe and Madagascar. Palaeontologists initially mistook its gliding rods for fin spines, and thought it was a fish.*

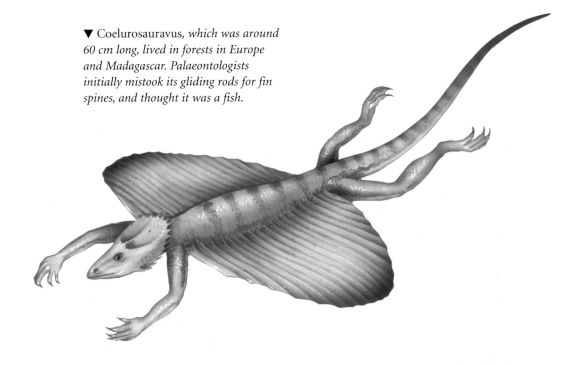

Rhamphorhynchoids

▶ Dimorphodon *had a wingspan of between 1.2 and 2.5 m. Palaeontologists think that it lived and hunted along seashores and rivers.*

- **The earliest pterosaurs** (flying reptiles) were the rhamphorhynchoids. They first appeared in the Late Triassic Period (around 220 mya).

- **Rhamphorhynchoids** had long tails that ended in a diamond-shaped vane, like a rudder.

- **Their tails** gave them stability in flight, which meant they could soar and swoop effectively.

- **One of the first rhamphorhynchoids** – and first flying vertebrates – was *Peteinosaurus*.

- **Well-preserved fossils** of *Peteinosaurus* have been found near Bergamo in Italy.

- **They reveal Peteinosaurus'** sharp, cone-like teeth, and suggest it ate insects, which it caught in the air.

- **In contrast**, another early rhamphorhynchoid, *Eudimorphodon,* had fangs at the front of its mouth and smaller spiked ones behind. This suggests that it ate fish.

- ***Dimorphodon*** was a later rhamphorhynchoid from the Early Jurassic Period (208–180 mya). It had a huge head that looked a bit like a puffin's.

- ***Rhamphorhynchus*** was one of the last rhamphorhynchoids, appearing in the Late Jurassic Period (about 160 mya).

▶ Rhamphorhynchus *had long, sharp jaws that it used to spear fish.*

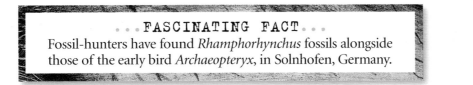

...**FASCINATING FACT**...
Fossil-hunters have found *Rhamphorhynchus* fossils alongside those of the early bird *Archaeopteryx*, in Solnhofen, Germany.

35

Pterodactyls

- **Pterodactyls** are a later group of pterosaurs (flying reptiles) than the rhamphorhynchoids.

- **They lived** in the Late Jurassic through to the Late Cretaceous Periods (160–65 mya).

- **Pterodactyls** lacked the long, stabilizing tail of rhamphorhynchoids, but were more effective fliers, able to make quicker turns in the air.

- **They were also** much lighter than rhamphorhynchoids, because their bones were hollow.

- **The pterodactyl *Pterodactylus*** and the rhamphorhynchoid *Rhamphorhynchus* were roughly the same size, but *Pterodactylus* weighed between 1 and 5 kg, while *Rhamphorhynchus* weighed 10 kg.

- **Some of the largest pterodactyls,** such as *Pteranodon,* appeared in the Late Cretaceous Period and had a wingspan of 7 m.

▶ Pterodactylus *was a small pterosaur that lived next to the sea. It fed on fish and shellfish.*

36

- **Unlike earlier flying reptiles**, *Pteranodon* had no teeth. Instead, it used its long, thin beak to scoop up fish.

- *Pteranodon* also had a pelican-like pouch at the bottom of its mouth – it probably used this to store fish before swallowing them.

- *Pteranodon* weighed about 16 kg. This was heavier than earlier pterodactyls, and suggests it was probably a glider rather than an active flyer.

- *Pteranodon* had a long crest on its head, which may have worked as a rudder during flight.

▼ Pteranodon, *meaning 'wings and no teeth', was once thought to be the largest ever flying reptile – until the discovery of* Quetzalcoatlus *in the 1970s.*

Quetzalcoatlus

- *Quetzalcoatlus* was the largest known flying animal of any kind ever to have lived.

- **It had a wingspan of 15 m** – the size of a small aeroplane!

- **It was also the heaviest** flying reptile, weighing 86 kg. Its bulk suggests that it was not a brilliant flyer, and instead glided as much as possible.

- **Its name** comes from an Aztec word meaning 'feathered serpent'. Quetzalcoatl was the Aztec god of death and resurrection.

- *Quetzalcoatlus* had long, narrow wings, jaws without teeth, and a long, stiff neck.

- **Palaeontologists** were amazed when they discovered the fossilized bones of *Quetzalcoatlus* – they did not think a flying creature could be that large.

- **The discovery** of these bones in inland areas, not coastal regions like those of other flying reptiles, suggests *Quetzalcoatlus* may have soared above deserts, like a vulture.

- **Some palaeontologists** say that *Quetzalcoatlus* was nothing like a vulture because its beak was not designed for ripping at the bodies of dead animals.

- **Another puzzle** for palaeontologists and mathematicians is how *Quetzalcoatlus* could lift itself off the ground to fly.

...**FASCINATING FACT**...
A student, Douglas Lawson, discovered *Quetzalcoatlus'*
bones in the Big Bend National Park, Texas, in 1971.

▼ Quetzalcoatlus *belonged to a family of pterosaurs called the azhdarchids,*
which had giant wingspans, long necks and toothless beaks. The name
'azhdarchid' comes from the Uzbek word for a dragon.

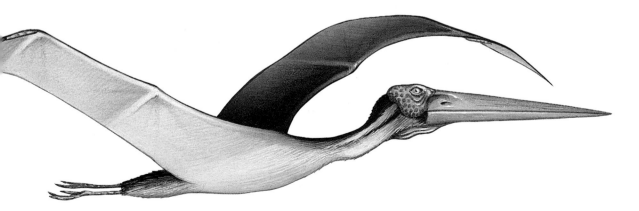

Index